Dog's Best Friend

More Citizen Dog Reflections

by Mark O'Hare

**Andrews McMeel
Publishing**

Kansas City

Citizen Dog is distributed by Universal Press Syndicate.

Dog's Best Friend: More Citizen Dog Reflections copyright © 1999 by Mark O'Hare. All rights reserved. Printed in the United States of America. No part of this book may be used or reproduced in any manner whatsoever without written permission except in the case of reprints in the context of reviews. For information write Andrews McMeel Publishing, an Andrews McMeel Universal company, 4520 Main Street, Kansas City, Missouri 64111.

99 00 01 02 03 BAH 10 9 8 7 6 5 4 3 2

ISBN: 0-8362-6751-6

Library of Congress Catalog Card Number: 98-88674

Cover illustration by Nick Jennings

www.uexpress.com

For My Family and Friends

A Review

B asically, there are just two types of books in the world.

The first type of book is the cat book. The cat book is a genuine and thought-provoking read. It employs subtle and inquisitive language to appeal to the hearts and minds of its audience. Its tone is patient, yet deliberate; the prose gently and craftily coaxes the reader through the narrative. The characters and story of a cat book are so entwined that readers scarcely realize themselves winding through the text. The cat book is a search for truth and meaning, a quest for identity. It emotes, it endears, it uplifts, and it endures.

And then, there is the dog book—meandering, impulsive prose that reads like a schnauzer holding up freeway traffic.

Cuddles Theodore Cat
literary critic, *The Cat's Meow*

TAP TAP TAP

C'MON! WHAT'S THE HOLDUP IN HERE?

I'M CONVINCED THAT WITH HUMAN BEINGS, EVOLUTION HAS GONE COMPLETELY BANANAS.

BURGERS AND HOT DOGS AND CHILI AND STEW! BADMINTON, LAWN DARTS AND TETHERBALL, TOO!

CALL UP YOUR FRIENDS AND YOUR NEIGHBORS AND YOUR OLD UNCLE LOU...

'CAUSE WE'RE GONNA HAVE US A BARBECUE!

OK! WHO WANTS THIS FIRST BABY?

PLORP!

6

"CAN YOU SEE ANYTHING?"

"BARELY."

"THEY ALL LOOK PRETTY FUZZY FROM UP HERE."

"WELL, WE HAVE TO MAKE DO WITH WHAT WE HAVE."

"YOU JUST KEEP TRACK OF ALL THE ACTION DOWN THERE AND WE'LL BE FINE."

"NOW LET'S START WITH THE PEANUT GUY. OK. HE'S NEAR RIGHT FIELD, THREE ROWS UP FROM THE MALT GUY. THE BEER GUY IS HEADING TO SECTION C..."

"HEY, BATTA, BATTA, BATTA!!!"

"SA-WING BATTA!!"

"YA THROW LIKE MY GRANDMOTHER, HERNANDEZ!"

"WOOOO!"

MUNCH CHOMP

SLURRRP!

"LOOK HOW MANY CHILI DOGS I CAN FIT IN MY MOUTH."

"COOOOL."

OZZIE'S AT THE PLATE. THERE'S THE PITCH...

WHOOP! HE POPS A FOUL. I WONDER WHOSE NAME IS ON THAT ONE!

PLOP!

WELL, WELL, WELL. THAT IS ONE LUCKY LITTLE FELLA!

WHAT AN INCREDIBLE GAME THIS HAS BEEN TONIGHT, BOB!

SNORE!

IT'S 12:30 A.M., AT THE TOP OF THE 13TH, WITH STILL NO SCORE. NO HITS, NO RUNS, NO NOTHIN'!

THERE'S NOTHING QUITE LIKE A WELL-PITCHED BALLGAME, BOB!

SNORE!

THIS IS TRULY ONE OF MOTHER NATURE'S FINEST SYMPHONIES!

FINEST WHATS?

SYMPHONIES. ONE OF MA NATURE'S FINEST.

YOUR MOTHER IS NO MUSICIAN, MEL.

NO, NO. MOTHER NATURE. AND I'M USING A METAPHOR TO—

SHE SURE IS A GREAT COOK, THOUGH. MMMM-MM!

HEY! I'M HUNGRY. LET'S GO GET A BURRITO!

15

18

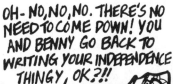

22

OK, OK. I'LL GIVE YOU **SEVEN** CENTS FOR THE JINGLE BALL. THAT'S MY FINAL OFFER.

THE PRICE IS **TEN**.

SEVEN!

TEN!

EIGHT!

ELEVEN!

NINE!

TWELVE!!

TEN!!

SOLD!!

NOW **WAIT** A MINUTE.

HELLO, BRUNO! DO YOU SEE SOMETHING YOU LIKE?

OH, GOOD CHOICE! YOU WANT THE COLLAR. WELL, THAT COSTS TWENTY CENTS.

TEN CENTS! IT COSTS TEN CENTS. MY MISTAKE. YOU ENJOY THAT COLLAR NOW, BRUNO.

YOU DON'T HAGGLE WITH BRUNO.

I'LL HAVE YOU KNOW THAT BECAUSE YOU WON'T GO BELOW TEN CENTS IN PRICE ON THE JINGLE BALL, YOU'VE LOST A VALUABLE PAYING CUSTOMER.

SO, HAVING SAID THAT, I'M LEAVING.

FINE.

AND I'M NOT COMING BACK.

OK.

GOODBYE.

SEE YA.

I HATE YOU.

27

DID YOU KNOW THAT THERE ISN'T ANYTHING ABOUT YOUR LIFE THAT MAKES SENSE TO ME?

NO, I DIDN'T.

WHIRRRRR

YEP. EVERYTHING FROM THAT GAS-GUZZLING SEDAN IN THE GARAGE TO THIS USELESS PASTA-MAKING WASTE OF TIME CONFUSES ME IMMENSELY.

WHIRRRRR

IN MY OPINION, YOUR SPECIES IS RAPIDLY DE-EVOLVING INTO FLESHY LITTLE PILES OF MINDLESS BIOLOGICAL GOO.

PHBBLTT!

JUST SO YOU KNOW WHERE I STAND.

I APPRECIATE YOUR HONESTY.

MOHARE

TWO CHEESE-BURGERS, A LARGE FRY AND A COLA.

PULL UP TO THE NEXT WINDOW, PLEASE.

MOHARE

WHAT'S THAT?

A DRIVE THRU.

SEE? YOU ASK FOR WHAT YOU WANT HERE, AND YOU PICK IT UP FROM THAT GUY OVER THERE.

NO KIDDIN'!

WORLD PEACE!

NO, NO. FROM THE MENU.

OH.

MOHARE

FIFTEEN CHEESEBURGERS...

...FIFTEEN JUMBO FRIES, FIFTEEN CHICKEN NUGGETS...

...FIFTEEN COLAS AND FIFTEEN VANILLA SHAKES!

AND AN APPLE PIE!

...AND AN APPLE PIE!

HELLO, BRUNO!

OH! THANK YOU.

HE GETS A LITTLE GIDDY LIKE THAT ONCE IN A WHILE.

FOR ME? THANKS!

31

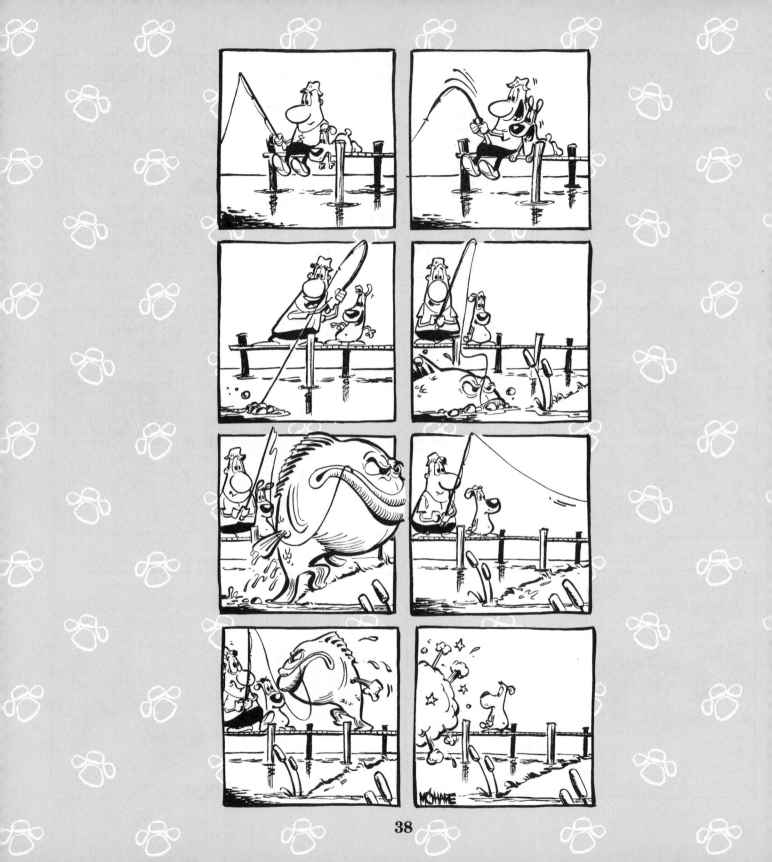

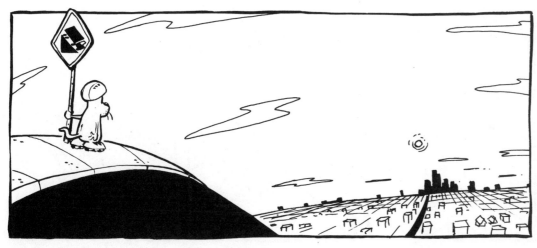

39

GISH!

OK. SO YOU PAINT THE EDGES LIKE THIS. UP, DOWN... UP, DOWN... UP, DOWN....

BUT I WANNA BE ROLLER GUY.

NOOO... I'M ROLLING. YOU'RE DOING THE EDGES.

NUH-UH. I'M ROLLER GUY. YOU'RE EDGE GUY.

I'M NOT DOING THE EDGES! GIMME THAT!

BACK OFF, EDGE GUY! BACK OFF, I SAID!!

I'M ROLLER GUY! SAY IT! SAY I'M ROLLER GUY!!

OK! OK! YOU'RE ROLLER GUY!

HEE HEE HEE HEE

HOW'S THAT ROLLING COMING ALONG?

JES' FINE.

TRY NOT TO GET ANY ON THE WINDOW, OK?

OKEEDOKEE.

HEH, HEH. THAT IS, IF YOU HAVEN'T ALREADY PAINTED OVER IT.

HEH, HEH, HEH. YEAH, RIGHT.

WELL... THERE IT IS.

YEP... THERE IT IS, ALL RIGHT.

ONE SLICE OF LEFTOVER APPLE PIE. I **KNEW** WE HAD SOME.

YEAH, I THOUGHT SO, TOO.

NOW THAT **THAT'S** SETTLED, MAYBE WE CAN FINALLY GET SOME SLEEP.

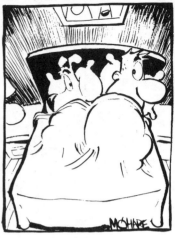

11:00 PM

1:00 AM

ZZZZzzzz

3:00 AM

5:00 AM

SNORRRE!

46

48

FOOMP!

OH, GOOD! THEY HAVE ONE MORE "GET SHORTY" LEFT.

YAAAAAAAAAAAAA

NO, NOT AGAIN. WE RENT THAT STUPID THING EVERY TIME WE COME HERE.

BESIDES, IT GIVES YOU AN ATTITUDE PROBLEM FOR AT LEAST A WEEK AFTERWARDS.

OK, EVERYBODY! IT'S TIME TO BOB FOR APPLES. WHO'S FIRST?

SPLOOSH!

AND THEN FRANKENTHTEIN THEZ, "HEY, DRACULA! WATCH WHERE YOU'RE THTICKIN' THOZ FANGS!"

AHHH-HA-HA-H HA-HA-HA-HA HA-HA-HA HA

WHOOP! IT LOOKTH LIKE MAH RIDETH HERE!

LETH DO THITH AGAIN REAL THOON, OK, FELLATH!

WOW! THAT'S THE MOON?

YEP.

IT DOESN'T SEEM AS STRANGE AND MYSTERIOUS WHEN I SEE IT THROUGH A TELESCOPE.

IT SURE ISN'T ANYTHING TO HOWL AT.

OH, JUST GREAT!! NOW YOU'VE RUINED IT FOR ME!!

HEY, BETTY! HOW ABOUT SOME REFILLS OVER HERE!!

REFILLS, BETTY!! REFILLS!!

DON'T YOU TWO HAVE JOBS TO GO TO?

HEY, MEL. WHAT'S A JOB?

I DUNNO.

I THINK IT'S LIKE WHAT BETTY DOES.

YESSS!

BONJOUR! JE M'APPELLE CHEF MEL.

...ET JE M'APPELLE CHEF FERGUS.

AUJOURD'HUI NOUS ALLONS PRÉPARER UN PEU DE CUISINE AMÉRICAINE, UNE VRAIE CLASSIQUE.

BEN... LA CUISINE AMÉRICAINE, LA CUISINE AMÉRICAINE... CHEF FERGUS, QU'EST-CE QUE C'EST QUE LA CUISINE AMÉRICAINE?

BEN...

"KRAFT MACARONI AND CHEESE"!

VOILÀ! LA CUISINE AMÉRICAINE!

IL FAUT FAIRE ATTENTION QUAND ON PRÉPARE LE "MACARONI AND CHEESE."

IL FAUT LAISSER BOUILLIR LES PÂTES DOUCEMENT DANS L'EAU. IL FAUT QU'ELLES RESPIRENT... IL FAUT QU'ELLES VIVENT.. VIVENT.

VIVE LE MACARONI!!!

VIVE LE MACARONI?!

C'EST TRÈS FRANÇAIS, N'EST-CE PAS?

Panel 1: BON, NOUS AJOUTONS LE FROMAGE, LE LAIT, ET LA BEURRE ET **VOILÀ** ... "MACARONI AND CHEESE"!

Panel 2: CHEF FERGUS, OÙ EST VOTRE **MOUSTACHE**?

MA MOUSTACHE?

Panel 3:

Panel 4: JE M'EXCUSE. "MACARONI, MOUSTACHE, AND CHEESE."

Panel 5: ALORS, CHEF FERGUS, EST-CE QUE VOUS AIMEZ LE "MACARONI AND CHEESE"?

PAS DU TOUT!

Panel 6: **NON**? VOUS N'AIMEZ PAS LE "MACARONI AND CHEESE"?

NON. JE NE L'AIME PAS.

Panel 7: POURQUOI?

Panel 8: IL LUI FAUT **DES WEENIES**!

VIVE LES WEENIES!!

Panel 9: LE "MACARONI AND CHEESE" C'EST **DÉLICIEUX**, N'EST-CE PAS?

OUI, OUI. C'EST **DÉLICIEUX**!

Panel 10: CHEF FERGUS, SAVEZ-VOUS CE QUI VA BIEN AVEC LA VRAIE CUISINE AMÉRICAINE?

NON, CHEF MEL. DITES-LE MOI?

Panel 11: UN BON **VIN AMÉRICAIN**. C'EST POUR ÇA QUE JE RECOMMENDE...

Panel 12: ..."BOONES FARM STRAWBERRY HILL, 1996." BON APPÉTIT!

ÇA A UN BON NEZ.

OK, FELLAS. WE'RE PARKED ON LEVEL G, SECTION 3. WE'LL MEET BACK HERE AT FIVE O'CLOCK SHARP. GOT IT?

SYNCHRONIZE WATCHES ... NOW!

—BOOP—

BEEP   BWEEP

LET'S SHOP!!

HMMM... CHEESE AND SAUSAGE GIFT PACKAGES. FERGUS MIGHT LIKE ONE OF THESE.

SMOKED SAUSAGE!

HICKO

THIS ONE'S A LITTLE SMALL. OH, HERE'S A PRETTY GOOD ONE... AND THIS ONE HERE IS A NICE SIZE. HMMM... WHAT TO BUY... WHAT TO BUY...

THE WISCONSIN BIG DADDY!

BELIEVE ME, THERE'S NOTHING ELSE QUITE LIKE THOSE VIBRATING FINGERS. IS THIS A CHRISTMAS GIFT FOR SOMEONE SPECIAL?

YEP.

RRRRR   RRR

WHY DON'T YOU COME WITH ME TO THE REGISTER AND I'LL SET YOU UP.

RRRRRRRR   RRR

RRRRRRRR   RRR

MY BUTT'S ASLEEP!!

RRRRRRRR   RRR

66

LOOKIN' GOOD, CUDDLES!

THANKS!

HEY, CUDDLES!

SSHHHK!

NEED A HAND?

ALL YOU NEED TO DO IS FIND YOUR BALANCE.

FIND MY BALANCE?

YEAH. FIND YOUR BALANCE.

FIND MY BALANCE...

APPARENTLY, IT'S IN MY FANNY.

79

SHOCK

DENIAL

ANGER

SADNESS

ACCEPTANCE

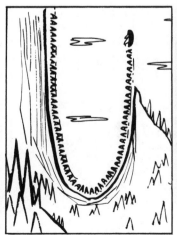

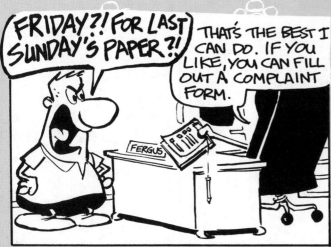

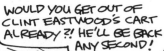

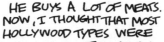

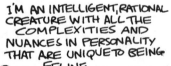

"CLAWS", THE CULTURALLY AMBIGUOUS CAT, HAS MADE A GRAVE MISCALCULATION OF HIS OPPONENTS' MASTERY OF BILLIARDS. PERHAPS HE HE HAS A CHANCE AT DARTS.

PFFT! PPPFFT! PFFT! PFFT!
PFFT! PFFT!

HOW'S LIFE IN THE FAST LANE, CLAWS?

PLEASE, JUST CALL ME CUDDLES.

SAY... YOU SEEN A CAT BY THE NAME OF "CLAWS" SLIP OUTTA HERE? HE OWES ME SOME DOUGH.

OH, YEAH. HE'S LONG GONE.

HE MENTIONED SOMETHING ABOUT SKIPPING TOWN. YOU MIGHT CATCH UP WITH HIM AT THE BUS STATION IF YOU HURRY.

IF YOU SEE THAT BUM TELL HIM HE OWES ME, TOO!

HE OWES ME BIG TIME.

SOOPERMART

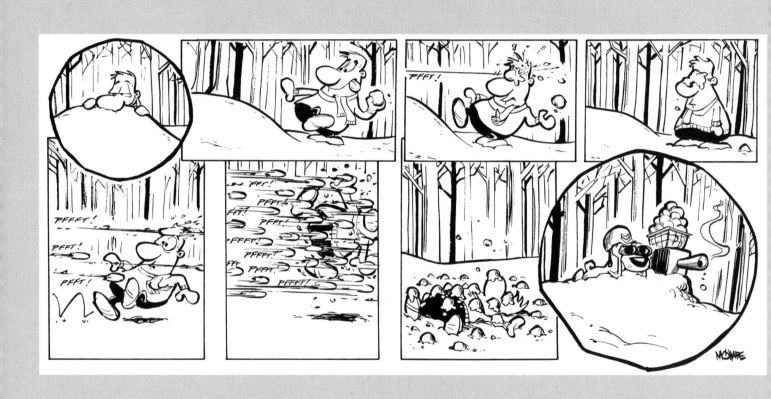

IS IT JUST ME OR DOES THAT GUY HAVE THE FATTEST HEAD YOU'VE EVER SEEN?!

BUM-BUM-BA-BOOM-DA-DOM-BUM-DUM-DA-DOOM-D

OPENS JUNE 3RD AT A THEATER NEAR YOU

WHAT AN AMAZING PREVIEW!

WOW!

...ACTION, ADVENTURE, ROMANCE AND DRAMA... ALL IN JUST 30 SECONDS.

A FILM HAS GOT TO BE PRETTY LOUSY TO REQUIRE A PREVIEW LIKE THAT.

WE'LL HAVE TO REMEMBER NOT TO SEE IT.

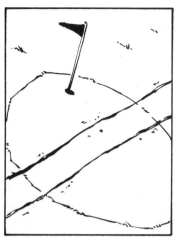

ÜBERSHMENKANVLAD!!!

WE DID IT! IT WAS A TOUGH ROAD, OL' BUDDY, BUT WE FINALLY FOUND THE LIVING ROOM WE WANTED....

OHHHH.... I'M SO HAPPY.

THIS STUFF IS **PERFECT** FOR THE DEN.

THAT CHAIR WOULD LOOK GREAT IN THE CORNER BY OUR TELEVISION.

AND THE COUCH COULD GO BY THE WINDOW.

WOW. IT'S A BIT PRICEY. THAT'S OK. WE CAN JUST GET WHAT WE CAN AFFORD.

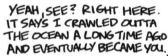

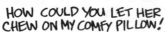

TIME FOR A SNACK RUN!

WHOSE TURN IS IT? I KNOW IT'S NOT MY TURN TO MAKE A SNACK RUN. IS IT YOURS, FERGUS?

NO, MEL. I DON'T THINK IT'S MY TURN EITHER. GEE, I WONDER WHOSE TURN IT IS?

LOOK OUT FOR THE ZOMBIE BRAIN SUCKERS!!! AHH-HA-HA-HA-HA-HA!

HA-HA-HA. VERY FUNNY, GUYS.

HERE HE COMES.

...BEING CHASED BY MUTANT ZOMBIE BRAIN SUCKERS, NO DOUBT.